College, Career & Money

A guide for Teens and Young Adults

Written by
Pastor Dave Burrows
and
Zhivargo Laing

Printed in the United States Of America

ISBN 0-9722625-4-7

Contents

Preface

Most teenagers have no plan for their lives. That's just a fact of life. Yet the most important thing in life at any age is to have a plan. Without advance planning results are unpredictable and distractions are inevitable. It is easy to focus on the wrong things if you don't plan properly. Most teenagers find themselves in this position, with no plan, so they get involved in a plan that someone else devised. Many times they don't know the origin or design of the plan but they end up living by it. They end up with AIDS, abortions, overdoses, incarceration and death and people keep wondering 'why?' The answer is that they have no plan. This book is a response to the need for planning and direction for the youth of today. I believe that if you take the challenge to read this book I guarantee you that your life will be changed for the better. The authors of this book have collectively dedicated their lives to guiding and directing youth in order that they may gain the maximum from their lives. It is the hope of both Minister Laing and Pastor Burrows that you, the young reader, would take full advantage of the information provided and use it to be the best that God created you to be.

Introduction

LIFE AFTER (High School) Graduation

Graduation is a right of passage. Counting both elementary, Junior High and Senior High, you have spent at least twelve years schooling. Now you prepare to move on. Up to this point, adults such as your parents and teachers directed your life. They told you when to rise, when to sleep, what to wear, what to eat, what to watch, what to read, when to slow down and when to put on speed. Their guidance sought to provide you with the best chance of receiving an education that would prepare you for life after graduation.

What was your school experience like? Did you get excellent, average or poor grades? Beyond the grades, did you get an understanding of the meaning of life and how to make the most of it? Did you learn how to act with emotional and social intelligence? No matter what your experience has been in school over the years, the time has come to move on. You must now move on, taking your experiences with you to help shape your future. Prior to now others structured your life, provided for you, sheltered and protected you. When you graduate you will be expected to do most of these things for yourself. What an exciting time this is! You should be beaming with anticipation, hope and desire. *Are you ready?*

Chapter 1

Preparing
for the
Future

1

Change is a prerequisite for progress. If something lives, it grows. If it grows, it changes. No progress occurs without change. Often, change is frightening. Graduation represents a major change for you and it can be scary. School has been a comfort zone for you for at least twelve years. You became used to the daily routine and experienced few uncertainties. You had few responsibilities. During your school years you had no bills and money was provided as needed, or in some cases, as wanted. However, after graduation life will be different. Many of the things that were done for you by parents, guardians and others you will now have to do for yourself. This is a major change and it can be unsettling. No matter how unsettling it is for you, it is time for you to move on.

What Do You Move On To?

Focus is critical to answering important questions. Focus is absolutely necessary at this time in your life. In fact, it is critical each time you must make important decisions. Focus means blocking out of your mind all unnecessary distractions, such as the TV, radio, certain internet sites, certain video games, certain parties and even friends. Once you remove distractions, you now set and keep your thoughts on getting answers to the questions before you. As you focus, you will find that there are really four basic options in moving on. They are discussed below.

Further Education

"Learning is not attained by chance; it must be sought for with ardor and attended to with diligence" (Abigail Adams). "Of making many books there is no end" (Eccl. 12:12). Learning never ends. You can continue your formal education in what are called tertiary (third) level institutions, such as universities (or colleges), training centers or technical schools. Tertiary institutions will later be discussed in detail. You can and should continue your intellectual growth through both informal and formal education. Formal education refers to schooling in a structured setting while informal education refers to more flexible everyday learning.

Self-Employment

Most people will work for others but self-employment is the wave of the future. You can, like others, start a business of your own. By using a trade or a practical skill learned while in school, you can sell a product or service that people value. This might include art, carpentry, plumbing, construction, computer programming, web design or electronics. Many College students have changed the world and become entrepreneurs simply by using simple skills learned in school. Some examples of these success stories include companies such as Google, Facebook and others that were started by teens or young adults. Perhaps your family has a business of which you can become a part. Self-employment is another good and mature option for you. There will be further discussion on self-employment later in this book as well.

Wasted life

Talents are meant to be multiplied. Sad to say, you do have the option of wasting your life when you graduate. This will happen if you don't work, pursue further studies or contribute positively to society. There may be a number of reasons why you, like others, end up wasting your life, but some of the more common ones include:

Lacking the patience to wait for what you want instead of expecting it immediately; being influenced negatively by others, including so called friends who decide to waste their lives; and participating in crime, violence, drugs, sexual deviance and other negative activities.

The Choice is Yours!

Choice is both a privilege and a responsibility. Control your choices and you control your world. What you choose to move on to is your choice. Where you go and where you end up will be the consequences of the choices you make right now. This right and privilege to freely choose what you will do with your life is also a major responsibility. Your choices will affect your destiny. What you choose today, you will look like tomorrow. Choose fat today; look fat tomorrow. Choose lean today; look lean tomorrow. Because choices are so powerful in influencing your future, you must make them wisely. Four keys to making wise choices are discussed below:

1) Seek Spiritual guidance.

"Trust in the LORD with all your heart and do not lean on your own understanding, in all your ways acknowledge him and he will direct your path."

As weird as it may sound, you cannot go wrong in your choices if you prayerfully consider them. Search the Scriptures for passages that relate to the issue that concerns you. You will find that the Bible has relevant historic and instructional truths on every matter that can concern you in this world. Also, consult a trusted counselor, teacher, coach, pastors and other trusted leaders. They can provide you with wise counsel. Sometimes it could be someone who has gone before you who you can learn from like a brother, sister, friend or parent.

2) Choice

Know what you really want. Good choices are easier to make when you know what it is that you desire most. It is important to spend quality time asking yourself questions about what you want to be; where you want to go; and what you want to do in life. Search for clear, realistic and practical answers. The answers you find will represent your personal goals in life. Once you know your goals, good choices will be those that help you achieve them.

3) Get as much information as possible.

To make good choices you need relevant information. This information includes:

All the alternatives and/or options;

The conditions attached to each alternative;

The consequences of choosing a given alternative;

Your expectations.

Information comes from listening to others, reading appropriate material, investigating the facts and examining and observing as much details as possible. In short, information comes from diligent search.

4) Seek good advice from knowledgeable people.

Making good choices often require advice. This advice can come from elders and persons who have expert knowledge of the area in which you must make a choice. Seek advice from such persons before you make your choices. Whether they are your parents, relatives, religious leaders, teachers or community leaders, they represent a rich source of guidance for decision-making. Make the choice that will make your life better, not worse.

The choice that will improve your physical, mental, spiritual and social life is the best choice. Choices that harm your body, mind, spirit or relationships with others are no good. People who make good decisions in their lives will testify to the benefits of the keys previously discussed. You would be wise to use these keys to unlock the door to your opportunities.

Mental Preparation and Planning

The slogan of the United Negro College Fund for years was "*A Mind is a terrible thing to waste*". The slogan was catchy and no doubt helped to raise millions of dollars for the education of young people, primarily of African descent. I am not sure who came up with the idea but it is absolutely imperative that as a teenager you develop a plan to determine what you will do with your mind. A mind is indeed a terrible thing to waste. It may be important to preserve your body but often the mind is the door to the body *and* soul and is strategically placed between them to direct what comes in and goes out. **Most of the major battles fought in the world today are for the minds of people, especially youth.** Every society that wants to change or any society that undergoes changes normally begins with an education program. Communists change a country with teachers first, then guns. Radical religious movements indoctrinate the minds of youth to become suicide bombers who carry out their philosophy of death and destruction. Your mind determines what your body will do; it determines whether you will do good or bad, whether you will end up in heaven or hell, the pit or the palace. The mind is a battlefield where many wars are fought and is a marketplace where ideas are sold and bought. Someone out there is after your mind because they know that if they can control your mind the battle is won. They can control you. Therefore you must have a plan for your mind.

There is a saying in computer terminology that states "Garbage in, garbage out". Your mind is a doorway, a storage tank and whatever you put into it is what you get out. Jesus, who was the greatest teacher, stated, "out of the abundance of the heart the mouth speaks", what is on the inside comes out of your mouth. You may wonder how I can develop a plan for my mind. Good question.

The plan for your mind begins with asking yourself who you want to be and whom you will serve in this life. Everyone in this life serves somebody, whether good or bad, we all serve someone. Your mind determines whom you will serve and what the results will be. Let's take the example of a typical country in the Western Hemisphere. The average salary of a high-school drop may be something like $15,000.00. The average high school graduate may be on average about $20,000.00 per year. The average college graduate may be $40,000.00 per year. The average Certified Public Accountant salary may be $60,000.00 and the list goes on. It pays literally to educate yourself.

The first item of mental preparation is to decide to educate yourself. Education is not an end, it is only a beginning. The example above shows that it is to your advantage to go as high as you can in the educational spectrum. It simply makes good sense to plan to continue your education at least to the college level. This does not mean that college or book education is the only type of education. You can also become educated in a trade that can earn you a lot of money and give you a very decent standard of living. The point is, however, that even in a trade area you must have the basics in order to succeed or gain the maximum success. **No matter how talented you are, if you cannot count or spell your own last name you are at a serious disadvantage in this world.** Many persons who fool around in high school and are real popular end up pumping gas for the rest of their lives or complaining that the government does not give them a job. Write your own ticket by educating yourself. Take advantage of school. Fun is important and has its place but do not let fun get in the way of your mental development. Get educated. Remember, the more you learn the more you earn!

Not only is education important for your future, it is also important to guard your mind from garbage. You may wonder, 'what do you mean by garbage?' Many young people today spend their time listening to and watching what could be called garbage. Most of the information on television, in the movies and on the radio is garbage (or unfruitful material that devalues). Much of today's music focuses on songs about sex and human body parts, a ladies behind or front, a man's crotch, violence, killing, cars, jewelry and in some cases utter stupidity if you really break it down. When today's artists are interviewed on television the standard reply is, "I am just singing about what is going on in society, in my hood". If this is the case, why don't they sing about *stopping* the violence or sing about how to respect a lady or something positive. The reason is garbage sells or people who make records believe that garbage sells. If you allow the perverted thinking of these people to be pumped into your mind every day the end result is that you develop garbage type thinking. Again you may ask how do I know. I know from experience. I (Pastor Dave Burrows) was one who watched, listened to and took in garbage all the time and my life began to be just like the songs I listened to. After much trouble, including being arrested by the police for marijuana possession, leading the police on a high speed chase and getting arrested for burglary and handgun possession, and various other legal problems, I decided to make a change and follow God's plan. I began to see that I could not listen to killing all day without it being on my mind when I sleep. I could not listen to sex songs all day and not be pre-occupied with sex. I could not watch these things and not have desires to follow at least some of the things I watched. Every television show, every movie and every song has a writer and producer. Producers and writers take their personal philosophy and put it into their songs, their movies and their shows in order to get you to agree with them. One example of this is soap operas. These are in most cases a demented reflection of life that warps the minds of many. How long can you sit and watch people hop from bed to bed, from marriage to divorce and not be affected in any way? Be careful what you watch. Be careful what you listen to because that is what you become. So I stopped listening to garbage and watching garbage. Violence and blood affect your mind. Decide to watch and listen to things that will make you a better person, increase your value and will help you fulfill your dreams. I have learned to listen to people with a positive message and watch things with a positive plot because I want to be better in life. My life has never been the same after I decided to cut out the garbage and to guard my mind and only let the good things in. The style is not the issue. The content and lifestyle of the artist or producer is.

Although formal education is of importance there is much you can do with your mind on your own without the assistance of school or teachers. The key is one four-letter word: **Read.** There is a vast array of information out there that you can take advantage of. Magazines on subjects that you are interested in can be a ticket to a career or may earn you money. **One of the things I have learned to do over the years is to read. Knowledge is power. Ignorance is a terminal illness. Knowledge is progress and ignorance is retardation. The more you read the more the world opens to you.** The more the world opens to you the more you can take advantage of opportunities.

Let me give you a personal example. I had no academic knowledge of computers. I had never studied computers in school but I educated myself to the world of computers by reading and asking questions of people who were already in the field. I read computer manuals, computer magazines and got information on the latest technology and equipment. Through my own diligence I ended up starting a computer school and computer company, selling computer products and earning a sizeable sum of money, just because I decided to read. Whatever your area of interest is it is important to read. Your best opportunities in life will come while you are young. You have time to read, time to experiment, and time to develop skills. When you get married your time is taken up largely by family concerns or paying bills. Use this time while you are still single to gain valuable information. Reading is the key.

While you are young you have the greatest opportunity to read good books and to listen to motivational cd's, DVD's or electronic material on important subjects. You also have the greatest opportunity to listen to positive music in whatever style you prefer because this is one of the keys in determining what enters your mind. Positive music builds up; negative music tears down.

Develop your Mind

Do what you can to gain the most from this world in influence, money and power in order to make **positive** contributions. Make yourself employable. If you want to get somewhere in life you must plan to educate yourself and pursue the career of your choosing. Remember to read books, magazines and other materials that are informative. Gossip magazines and corrupt novels will not give you the desired result. A clear mind allows you to be the best lawyer, accountant, doctor, farmer, fisherman or computer analyst you can be. Develop your Mind by learning all you can learn.

Chapter 2

Seizing OPPORTUNITIES

According to Henry David Thoreau, "The world is but a canvas to our imagination."

You must determine within yourself to paint that canvas with your dreams.

Go for it!

Webster's New American Dictionary defines opportunity as a favorable combination of circumstances, time and place; a chance for advancement. Many opportunities remain untapped. As a result, many people fail to realize their dreams. It is easy to think that opportunities exist everywhere but where you are. 'If only I lived in another city, state, town, somewhere in another country or another city or town, you might say to yourself, then I would stand a better chance.' It is true that highly developed communities offer many opportunities to prosper. However, did you notice how many Americans, Englishmen and Canadians live, work and conduct business in other countries? There are thousands. Why? They find enough opportunities in The Bahamas or other parts of the world to leave their own countries to go where you live. They find success in your own country or community that many of you miss. They use their savings, knowledge, expertise and skills to take advantage of opportunities that exist right there in your hometown. You can be just as enterprising as them. Indeed, you can be even more enterprising than they.

There are opportunities *everywhere*. If you are focused, observant, diligent and patient you can take advantage of them for your own good and the good of others. Some of these opportunities exist now, some will come later and some you can create.

Existing opportunities

Existing opportunities include continuing education and training; or employment or business, tourism, financial services, wholesale and retail trades, construction, fisheries, agriculture, information technology, auto mechanics, carpentry and other trades. There are also opportunities to become a leader in business, religion, education, civics, and local or national politics.

Some people believe that the areas just mentioned have all the people they need. Perhaps a story will help answer this point. One day a prominent leader was asked if he thought that there were too many lawyers in his community. He responded "It is true that there are many lawyers but there is always room for more **good** lawyers". The point is this, **if you aim to excel instead of being average in any area, there will always be room for you.**

Coming opportunities

The world is in a constant state of change. Progress is always being made. As political, social and economic conditions in the world improve, more and more opportunities will come, both nationally and internationally. The expansion of private enterprise and Government programs will also bring new opportunities. Some examples of persons who have created their own opportunities include Bill Gates of Microsoft and Steve Jobs of Apple Computers. As young persons they did not wait on a job, but used their creative skills to produce ideas and products that literally changed the world. Why can't you do the same? As local businesses expand and additional foreign investments takes place economic opportunities will be created. This will mean new jobs, new skills, new capital and greater exposure. Areas that you are interested in may not now offer much opportunity but they may come later as your community continues to develop. Be ready for these opportunities. Do not wait until they come before making preparations. In the Bahamas, where I am from, some areas expected to blossom in the future include:

Ecological Tourism
Marine Farming
Maritime Businesses
Electronic Commerce

Created opportunities

You don't need to wait on opportunities; you can make some happen.

You are as talented and full of potential as anyone in the world. You may decide to use your talents to make good things happen for you and others. You can create opportunities for educating yourself and others; for making money; for improving neighborhoods, and for helping your community to become a better place. Through creativity, hard work and persistence you can materialize these opportunities.

If you are a teenager today I would like to ask you a few honest questions.

#1. Would you like to end up in jail?

#2. Young lady, would you love to get pregnant and have three children before the age of seventeen?

#3. Would you, as a teenager, love to catch AIDS and die?

#4. Would you love to overdose on Cocaine and die?

#5. Would you love to be shot to death or stabbed to death as a young gang member? Would you?

If you are normal you would probably say to yourself, 'what kind of drugs can you be on to even ask a question like that? You should know teenagers don't want any of these things to happen to them.' Although this is the normal reaction the truth is teenagers end up in jail all the time. Many get pregnant before the age of seventeen. Many end up HIV positive and many die of drug overdoses every year. Many more die a violent death due to gang violence or teen crime. Statistics indicate that teen crime, teen pregnancy, teen violence, AIDS among teenagers and teen drug abuse are at unacceptable levels. In fact in some areas and some countries the teen problems are being called epidemics, and have never been seen before on the scale we are witnessing today.

The question is if most teenagers do not want to end up in the positions outlined above, why does it keep happening? Why is it that wherever I travel in this world teenagers tell me they never want to be in any of these positions yet when I listen to the news or return to a town for a visit inevitably their friends come up to me and say, "so and so is in jail", 'so and so is pregnant' (or had a baby), 'so and so had an abortion', 'so and so is on drugs'. Why?

There are many reasons. **The world we are living in today is crazy, mixed up, sometimes stupid, confused and anything else you can think of. This world is messed up in many ways.** It is especially so for teenagers. Families can't stay together, governments are making irrational decisions, blacks are killing blacks, Hispanics are killing Hispanics, there's violence on TV, violence is on the movie screens, and violence and sex are in the music. Something is desperately wrong with society as a whole. Something is wrong with the whole world as a matter of fact. There are many factors we can look at and many people we can blame. If teenagers blamed their parents or the elders of society they would be partially right, but as a teenager if you are right in blaming everybody else that still does not help you. You still have to deal with this world and you still have to find your way in this jungle. You still have to seize the opportunity.

Most young people fail and end up being destroyed because they lack a plan for their lives. They lack vision. Most adults are not good at planning either, but we have this especially in teenagers. Most teenagers live by the day. *"Where is the party this weekend? Why didn't she call me? Where can I get my next high or my next good time? What's happening? Where's the party?"* Let's face it, if you are a teenager you probably don't wake up in the morning worrying about the budget deficit. You probably don't think much about world famine or civil wars or tribal wars or the price of oil or things adults sit in front of the TV and get ulcers worrying about. Your concerns are in most cases for today, things happening in your immediate world. This is the very thing that can kill you, just being concerned about today. You don't plan to fail, but you fail. Why? Because you don't seize the opportunities available to you.

You may ask me 'what do you know about this stuff? You are an adult, how do you know what we have to deal with,' or 'what makes you an authority on this subject?' Good questions. That's the reason why we wrote this book. You see for many years of my life I (Pastor Dave) had no plan, or should I say, I did not have the *right* plan. Someone came along and introduced me to drugs at the age of twelve and by the time I was thirteen I was selling drugs in school and on the street. I stayed in trouble in school and often got kicked out for doing dumb things, like robbing other students, cussing teachers, throwing a teacher on the ground, fighting and everything else. I stole from the food store, stole from the bank, sold drugs at night, hung with notorious gangsters and ended up in police custody just barely missing a long sentence on two occasions and ending up on probation. I know what it is to not have a plan and end up living by the plan of the street or the plan of 'let's go', 'let's do this', 'let's do that'. I know what I am talking about and fortunately I lived to tell about it. Some of my old friends cannot talk about it anymore. They are gone.

When I developed the right plan for my life, things changed. I began, through God's help, to control my own destiny. I became the leader instead of the one being led. So I know what I am talking about. I lived without a plan and I also lived with the right plan. It's better to live with the right plan.

One fact of life is that most people in the world are unintentional losers. Most teenagers are under achievers. I know you want to jump in my face over a statement like that but let me qualify it. Very few people achieve their dreams in life. Very few live above what they expect. **A winner is one who hits his targets, who sets his standards higher, who has goals and plans and who leads others**. Most people in the world are ordinary; followers who follow instructions and look for answers. Leaders create instructions for people to follow and answer the questions that others ask or complain about. Most winners have a plan that goes beyond the next party or next week. That is why I say the majority of the world is filled with unintentional losers; they live below what is available to them. They settle for less than what they can achieve. Planning separates winners from losers. Winners seize opportunities.

Seeing Ahead

In deciding to seize opportunities you must know the basics of planning. There is a system of planning that needs to be learned in order to get the most of your planning exercise. Whenever a house is being built before anything is done on the site a plan is drawn detailing where everything will be; toilets, light fixtures, the room for Johnny, Susie's room, the TV room and so on. This is done long before you start building the house. Even after it is done, before you can start building the plan has to be taken to the proper authorities for approval.

This is a key in planning for teens. Submit your plans to someone who is an authority. It may be your parents, if you have a close relationship, or your guidance counselor, youth pastor or your pastor.

Make sure the person you submit your plan to is trustworthy and legitimate. Ask them for advice. You may want to talk to more than one person. Listen to their advice and like the architect, gain the necessary approvals. In whatever you do, your conscience and your personal convictions are still your guide. Plans can change or be altered but it is always necessary to begin with a plan.

Planning should be done to cover three areas of your life (Spirit, Mind and Body) for the periods (first 25 years, second 25 and third 25 year periods).

All of us are made up of three parts. *Spirit:* which is the real you, *Soul:* which includes your intellect and emotions and *Body:* which is the physical house that houses the other two parts of you. **It stands to reason then that we must plan for these three areas of our lives.** Some people only plan for their body, especially good athletes, so their minds suffer. If they get injured they become permanent losers in life. Imagine if a potential NBA star got injured at the age of seventeen and put all his hopes in his athletic career. He could end up a "dumb" good athlete. If he planned for his mind, however, and he failed with his body his future would not be lost. If as a young person you have no plan for your spirit then you may achieve fame and fortune only to die a fool. The Bible notes, "What profit is it to gain the whole world and lose your soul (Mark 8:36)". **It is a must then that your plan for your life includes Spirit, Soul and Body.**

In addition to planning for the three areas of your life you should also plan for the three periods of life. What are the three periods of life? To put it in a simple fashion let's call it the **Me** period, the **We** period and the **Them** period. In most developed countries people live at least until the age of 75 on average. This is not a completely hard and fast rule but for the sake of simplicity, lets divide your life into three parts.

The first third is the first 25 years of your life. During the first third of your life you should concentrate on you. Develop everything related to you. Work on your spirit, soul and body. Pursue your career goals, get your education finished with and get a substantial job. Many young people take too much time in the first 25 years of life focusing on others, a boyfriend or girlfriend and end up in relationships that deprive them of personal development. **You could save yourself a lot of hassle by not getting into any serious relationships until you are in your early twenties and in the process of completing your educational, career and personal goals.** Use this time of your life to develop your talents, learn to play a musical instrument, develop your athletic skills, pursue your career goals, learn a trade, pursue your spiritual goals or become a leader in your school, church or civic group. Once you have done these things then you are ready for the next phase of your life.

The second phase of your life is the time when you are ready and able to take care of a family; the **We** phase. This second twenty-five year period should be devoted to developing your family. By this time you should have already completed your formal education and settled into a good job and career. You should have sufficiently developed yourself during the first stage to the point where you can focus your attention on your wife or husband and the family that will come out of your union. Once your personal priorities and career are under control it is a lot easier to care for a family and build a secure home environment for them. Many people who have not developed sufficiently before taking on a spouse end up with a lot of unnecessary difficulties because they failed to prepare themselves for the second phase of life. Focus on providing for the physical, emotional and spiritual needs of your family during this stage.

The third phase of your life is the **Them** phase. Once you have developed yourself personally and have taken care of your immediate family, as you get older you can focus in on the next generation, the *them* stage. In the same manner your early years should prepare you for what is to come in terms of getting married and raising a family, the later years should be geared toward leaving a deposit in the generation just beginning. When you have reached over fifty, life may still be fun and things may be wonderful, but you are definitely on the way toward the grave. This is a cold statement but it is still true, the older you get the closer you are to the grave. If you know that you will be leaving eventually, it is then important to leave your wisdom with those just beginning the process. Focus your attention in your later years on the young ones who will be just learning about life. The wisdom of years of living can be a vital source of information for the young.

What I have outlined here is just a pattern. It is not an absolute but it is a guide you can follow as you plan for your life ahead. As I stated earlier it is much better to have a plan than not to have one. Plans may change or be altered but a plan is far better than no plan. **You can only seize opportunities when you have planned.**

Chapter 3

Going to College?

Pursuing higher education is exciting. Expanding the mind beyond the knowledge of high school offers power. This power can be used to achieve success in life. You can further your formal education in college, university, a technical institute or training program. Completing tertiary training can provide you with any or all of the following:

Associates Degree
Bachelors Degree
Master Degree
Doctorate/Ph.D.
Specialized Certification

The Associates Degree is a degree obtained after about two years of college instruction. The Bachelor Degree can be a Bachelor of Arts (BA) or a Bachelor of Science (BS); each is obtained after three or four years of tertiary level instruction and are referred to as first degrees. The Masters degree is obtained after the Bachelors degree, following about two additional years of college education and usually in a concentrated subject. The Doctorate or Ph.D. is the highest level of tertiary education one can obtain. It normally requires at least one additional year of college instruction following the Masters, along with intense research in a concentrated area. Both a Masters and Doctorate can be obtained in either the Arts or Sciences.

You can choose to further your formal studies both at home or abroad. Both options should be considered carefully. Sometimes it is advantageous to complete your entire studies at home. At other times you can do a part of your studies at home and the remainder abroad. There are many advantages to studying at home. Primarily, it is less expensive and serves as excellent preparation for further study should you decide to go abroad. Also, the schools within your community may offer a level of quality comparable to many outside institutions. You will benefit tremendously by beginning your tertiary education at home. The choice of studying at home or abroad depends upon a number of factors. These factors include:

Availability of courses - You can only choose to study at home if the local institutions offer the particular field of study in which you have an interest and offers it at the level you desire. If, in your locale, one cannot obtain a Bachelors degree in Physics or Mathematics and this is your area of interest, then studying abroad is the only option. However, a Bachelor of Arts in Education can be obtained from almost any institution.

Availability of funds - Generally speaking, it is less costly to study at home than it is to do so abroad. This is usually the case because local institutions have state subsidy for tuition and you can save on room and board, since you can live at home. If funding is a challenge for you, studying at home might be a more attractive option.

Other factors - There can be other reasons for choosing to study at home or abroad, including one's age, medical circumstances, immigration status or scholarship requirements.

STUDYING ABROAD

Exposure to another culture or country provides knowledge about the diversity of our world as well as an appreciation of the beauty of your home country.

Perhaps you want to go to another town or state or even overseas to study. This can be a beneficial experience. Thousands have studied abroad, mostly in North America (USA and Canada) and Europe (England and France). Sometimes getting an opportunity to study abroad can seem impossible, as funds may be low, qualifying may seem difficult and just getting through the application forms may appear complicated. Still, you can do it! Be patient. Seek the help of those who have been through that experience. Here are the basic steps you should take in pursuing studies abroad.

Know what you want to study.

Some school programs in a given field are better than others. If you know what you want to study you can then choose the best schools for your specific field of study and can seek advice from capable people (guidance counselors, parents, career persons, pastors, etc.). It is not uncommon though, that you may go to school without knowing exactly what you want to do. This should not cause undue concern because the first two years of college are general studies and you can use this time to choose a specific field of interest.

Know your academic qualifications.

Face the facts. Some colleges and universities have higher standards than others. They require a high Grade Point Average (GPA) from high school and numerous outstanding accomplishments. If you do not meet the criteria of a given school, then you are not likely to get into that school. The fact that you graduated from high school, though, means that you should be able to get into some institute of further learning. Once in the institution, you can work on improving your academic standing.

Know what your overall GPA is for high school.

Know what academic certificates you hold and with what grades. Know what special accomplishments you have, athletic or otherwise. Keep note of any clubs or special activities you have been involved in, this may be a selling point for some schools. You should be able to prove that you possess the certificates that you claim to have or the accomplishments you made. Know your talents and hobbies.

Visit your school's counseling office.

Talk to your guidance counselor about your desire to attend college. He or she should have a number of college or university reference books, application forms or brochures on hand. Your counselor should also be able to direct you to many websites of appropriate colleges. The guidance counselor should also be able to give advice about choosing a school and filling out necessary forms. It is important to find out the deadline for applying to given schools because if you apply too late you may not be considered for the semester of your choice. Additional places to find out about various colleges are the library, the Internet, and books such as a comprehensive college reference or guide. The Internet is especially good in today's world as you can access just about any college campus you are interested in and even fill out applications online.

Complete application forms and submit on time.

You may want to sit with someone who has been off to school in order to complete the college application forms. Such forms can often be complex and can be seen as part of the college's entrance test. After all, if you are unable to complete the form, it is highly unlikely that you will be able to survive in the college. It is very important to seek help; seeking help is an example of being intelligent.

Once the application forms have been completed, send them off in adequate time to allow them to arrive at the colleges long before the deadline. You should consider that a form could take about two to three weeks by regular mail and if you can afford to do so, you should send the forms via express mail, UPS or Fed Ex, particularly if you are pressed for time. Send applications to as many colleges as possible but be aware that you will be charged a non-refundable application fee. This fee varies from one college to the next. Some agencies allow you to apply to several colleges at once, thus reducing the expenses involved. It may also be possible for you to apply online for some schools. For more information you may check with a guidance counselor. Some colleges allow you to apply online as well.

Prepare to sit required exams.

Colleges normally require that you sit certain proficiency examinations as part of the entrance requirement. For the USA and Canada, such exams include the SAT (Scholastic Aptitude Test), ACT, TOEFL, etc. You will probably only have to sit the SAT. The UK requires that you have acceptable passes in GCE O' levels and A' levels or the BGCSE. Again, check with your guidance counselor for test dates and details. Scores achieved on the examinations will have to be directly forwarded from the schools to the institutions to which you have applied

If you will need financial assistance, you must seek out various scholarships well in advance. Most communities have an extensive listing of available scholarships with requisite application forms. There are also private scholarships offered which you may seek out by looking in the newspapers, online, checking with various business houses, checking with the

Chamber of Commerce or just asking around. The schools to which you apply may offer financial aid to certain students as well. You should apply for such aid if you feel you meet the qualifications. Finally, some foreign embassies also offer a number of undergraduate scholarships and exchange programs. You can search the Internet for contacts and speak with your guidance counselor. If you must, you may also wish to seek private sponsorship from willing individuals such as friends and relatives.

When you first apply to a school, you may not be accepted. Do not be discouraged. Try again next year. In the meantime, prepare yourself for the next time you apply to the college of your choice. You can work and save some money or start a program at home and continue it overseas when the opportunity presents itself again. Don't give up! Keep trying.

Former Teachers Help.

Your teachers have been tremendous help to this point. I know that they were paid to teach you but they were not paid to do the extras that most of them did. They gave advice, came in for extra classes, prayed for you, and more. You should continue to be in touch with them and when necessary, seek their help. Also, it would be a good idea to find out from them if you can be of some help to them as they do their jobs. All teachers have some College experience so they are an excellent resource.

Community Leaders Help.

Religious, civic, business and political leaders can be sources of help. They can offer advice, information, jobs, scholarships, etc. You should know how to contact them and use their help where it is available.

Fellow Graduates Help.

The people who you graduate with can also be sources of help. They can team up with you to find jobs, colleges, volunteer groups and business opportunities. Stay in touch with as many of your friends as possible especially those in your field of study.

Family's Help.

Your parents or guardians have done much to get you to this point in your lives. They have spent time, effort and money to give you the opportunity for an education. Every dollar they spent on you was a dollar they could not spend on themselves. Now that you are finished with school, you should not abandon them. You should grow even closer to them. You will not continue to depend on them as you did before, but you will need their moral and emotional support and they will need yours. Take time to thank them for their help and to seek that help when you really need it. They love you and will continue to encourage you. Hopefully, as a result of your success, you will be in a position to help them some day.

Help rarely comes automatically.

Often times you must ask for it. So don't sit still waiting for someone to help you. Go and find the help you need. When you reach out for help and that help is not available; don't stop looking. Try someone else or somewhere else. Do not be thin-skinned; be diligent. You will find the help you need eventually.

Keep Believing

I must mention here the important of using your faith and believing in spite of the odds. You should always respect, depend on and believe that there is hope beyond what we can see. Someone has been helping you all this time to make it in life. If you are a person of faith and prayer, pray and spend time with those who you believe are like-minded for support. All things are possible if you just believe.

Keep Working

Work as if there is no help to be found so that if help does not come you will know how to work without it. However, if help does come it will only add to the effort you are already making.

Although things will not always be easy, you do have help. Smart people accept help when it is available. The help that is available to you comes from many different sources.

Finally, you must help others. Too many people in this life just take. We need people to give also. A famous Bible verse states, " It is more blessed to give than to receive". Make yourself available to help others no matter who they may be.

OTHER CHALLENGES

If you do not have the minimum entry requirement for the institution of your choice, speak with the academic dean of the institution to find out what you can do to enter in the future. Take courses in order to pass the required exams (SAT, etc.). There are computer programs and online sites that you can purchase that can prepare you for these exams. You can go over these programs again and again until you feel you have improved your preparation. If all else fails find another institution that will accept you and work hard to improve your academic standing.

Remember that two of the most important decisions you will ever make in your life are choosing a College and/or choosing a Career. Why are these decisions so important? **Because you will probably spend more of your time in life on a job than any other single activity.** It is important to spend this vast amount of time doing something you love and doing something that is profitable. If you make the wrong choices you can end up doing something you hate and at the same time making less money than you would like. The end result is a lifetime of misery and under achievement. It is important to make the right decisions early in order to preserve yourself from the heartache that comes from regrets. Don't be left saying, "If only I had done this or if only I had decided earlier". The Ball is in your court. Here are some suggestions to help you with some of the decisions you will face:

Selecting the Right College:
Price:

Since economics play a big role in all of our lives it is important in se-
lecting a college to know the cost of tuition, accommodation, food and
all the other aspects of college life. You do not want to shortchange
yourself on quality but neither do you want to bite off more than you
can chew. Perhaps you can get the same education at a less expensive
institution. Weigh the cost versus the benefit in order to make a good
selection.

New Cultures:

Another consideration that will help you with your college choice and in
preparing for college is to know the culture of the city or country where
you will be going to school. Cultural differences are very important and
it helps with your adjustment to college life if you are aware of cultural
differences. The first year of college is often the most difficult and you
can make the transition easier if you are aware of the culture of the city
or country and college. In your first year of college you are away from
home, like so many others, and there are no parents to watch you or
correct you. Therefore, be careful not to throw away the values you have
learned all your life just because others are doing so. Evaluate the good
and bad of your new environment.

Paying for College:

This is one of those nagging questions that never seem to have a simple
answer. If you have rich parents it is a simple matter. If you don't it is not
so simple. Here are some things to consider:

Even if your parents can afford it, it is important to make contributions
to your own education. This is the responsible thing to do. Making a
contribution to your education increases the value of it to you and begins a valuable lesson that will be important for years to come. In some
cases there are banks that may offer loans based upon the profession
you are pursuing. Some banks will offer loans for the medical profession

or professions that are very likely to earn high income in later years. In some cases your family may take out a revolving loan that is renewed each year as necessary. In some cases you may want to work for a year or two then go to school, or you may have the opportunity to work part-time while you are in school.

College Online

One very interesting trend that can have a major impact on how we attend College is the emergence of online schools or schools with online options. One of the most popular of these schools is the University of Phoenix. These schools allow you to stay at home and actually do your college courses online. This can significantly reduce costs and make college much more affordable. There are pros and cons for this option as you will have to be self disciplined and you will not have the college community experience. One thing for sure is that you can save money. Most major colleges now have an online option so this is worth exploring if cost is an issue and you are a person who can work on your own.

Scholarships:

There are numerous scholarships offered to students who excel academically. Although there is intense competition for these scholarships any scholarship you can obtain is a positive contribution to your education. One scholarship that has to be considered and planned for early in your life is a talent scholarship. Many schools offer a variety of talent-oriented scholarships. Sports is a very big area and if you are talented in any sport it makes good sense to get the most out of your talent. A basketball, football, baseball or tennis scholarship can be worth up to $200,000.00 or more over a four-year period. There are tremendous sacrifices that you will have to make in terms of practice and travel but this can be considered the 'price' of your free education. Other talents can also be important. For example, music is another area that can bring great benefit. Many schools offer music scholarships if you are talented in this area. The same goes for dance, drama and a number of other disciplines. It seems, however, that sports scholarships are the surest ticket. Whatever the case may be, take advantage of any scholarship within your reach.

Relationships & College

Another area of important consideration if you are on your way to college is relationships. Many times you may have a girlfriend or boyfriend at home before you go to college. Sometimes the relationship may be very serious or just somewhat serious. If you are going to college, my belief is that the best thing to do is to put relationships on hold unless you are planning to attend the same school together. **One of the most difficult things to do in life is to conduct a long distance relationship. It costs in terms of phone bills, it is difficult to resolve conflicts over the phone or on the internet and one of the persons in the relationship is likely to feel tied down, especially after discovering the wider world of college life.** I believe it is important to explore new relationships, to make friends and to take your time before getting into serious relationships. College is a time of growth and transition. Help to make it a smooth one by not committing yourself emotionally. Some people already know what they want and can go to college together, get married and achieve their education together. This is unlikely but it is not impossible. It is up to your good judgment to explore the ins and outs, receive counsel and ponder the advice you get before making a decision.

Knowing the Community:

When choosing a college it is important to know the community you are going into. Learn about the culture and the environment of the area you are going to. It is good even to know the weather of the area since you will be spending several years of your life there. Personally I hated cold weather but ended up in a cold weather environment. This may or may not be a big factor in your decision- making but it is important. You should also determine if there is a church or organization in the community that would help with your spiritual development. Perhaps you can speak with your advisor and get his recommendation for the area where you are going.

Fraternities & Sororities

Inevitably the question of fraternities and sororities will arise when it comes to college. My personal opinion is to be very careful about these organizations. Some have excellent programs while others focus in on partying and in some cases alcohol and drugs. Research the background of each one from your personal belief system and decide based upon your convictions. Some people from a Christian perspective stay away from these organizations because of a clash of values. Research entry requirements and find out whether you will be asked to 'pledge' to things that are in conflict with your values. Be extra careful about hazing rituals that involve degrading behavior. In some cases these activities require dehumanizing rituals that in some cases have led to personal injury and even death. There have been numerous stories of wild parties, excessive drinking, violence and general mayhem with "some" fraternities in particular. While there are some of them that have higher standards and provide positive activities, many are involved in alcohol abuse as well as wild partying. The decision on a matter like this should be based upon your own values and those of people you trust. Talk to your parents before making critical decisions. If no parent is available, talk to a trusted counselor or advisor.

College Temptations:

Always remember that college is a great opportunity for growth but it is also a great opportunity to succumb to loose or slack moral standards and sexual promiscuity. College campuses are in many cases a haven for experimentation and an escape from parental restrictions. It is important not to throw away restraints and principles you have grown up with because you are in college. Whatever your standards are, maintain them. Standards are a guide for all of your life, not just one period. These standards cause you to win in life, not just for a period of time or an occasion. Make sure you set standards for others rather than having them set standards for you. Unfortunately, my first college experience was full of drugs, partying and wild uncensored activities. I ended up being arrested and put on probation, almost being sentenced to three years in jail because of throwing off restraints and just living like I felt.

Chapter 4

Other
Learning
Options

Jr. (Community) College or Major College:

If money is an issue, or if you feel you need a year or two to make the transition to a major college, a Junior or Community College is an option. Many times a Junior College is much less expensive than a four-year institution, very flexible and most of your credits can be transferred to the college you plan to attend. Make sure you check to see if your credits will be accepted before you enroll, otherwise your time and money will be wasted. You may also want to consider earning an Associates Degree first then pursuing a Bachelors Degree.

TECHNICAL AND VOCATIONAL INSTITUTES

These institutions provide training for immediate employment and offer a large number of certificate programs including Air Conditioning and Refrigeration, Arts and Crafts, Auto Body Repair, Auto Electric, Auto Mechanics, Business Studies, Carpentry, Cosmetology, Dressmaking, Electrical Installation, Electronics, Joinery, Masonry, Painting and Decorating, Tailoring, TV and DVD repair and Welding. Additionally, you are exposed to Blue Print Reading, Math, Entrepreneurial Skills, Communication skills and computers. Each of these areas represents a trade that is in great demand in today's world. With training in any one of these areas you will be well on your way to dignity, self respect, wealth and success. With these institutions you can receive Seminar Certificates, Training Certificates and Diplomas in your desired field.

Specialty schools:

Some of you may be saying, 'Yeah but what if I don't want to go to college? I know the area I am interested in and there are schools that offer professional certification that are not colleges.' That is fine. If you are interested in a career in the recording industry there are schools that deal specifically with that industry. The same applies to fields like Culinary Arts, Cosmetology, mechanics and numerous other industries. Take advantage of what is out there in these areas if it is your desire. A four-year college is not a must. Professional certification can be just as rewarding financially, especially if it is in a field that you prefer working in and are strong in.

Career VS Hobby:

Do not make a career decision solely based on what you like or are good at because some things you are good at may need to be pursued as a hobby rather than as a career. Suppose you are talented at **art** but also have an interest in **business.** Perhaps you can pursue business as a career; art as a hobby and perhaps the art can grow into a business. There are some things you do for love or personal enjoyment and other things you do for money.

Formal and Informal training:

Sometimes you may be better off taking a course in a skilled area than in going to a four-year college. If you have a specialty you may end up going to a school for a year or two for specific study in your field of interest. A one or two year course in computer repairs may end up being just as beneficial as a four-year college degree. Many schools offer specialty training in given fields. Some of the courses include computers, music, various technologies, mechanics, electronics, sewing, electrolysis, cake baking and cosmetology. There are countless others. In addition much of your training can be informal by working with a professional in the area you are interested in. Informal education from someone with experience can be a great asset also. The little things you may learn from a tradesman like a carpenter, mason or plumber may end up being of great value to you later in life, especially when you own a home and things break down or even when you are building your own home. Use every opportunity to learn skills for the future. Little things can mean much in the long run.

Continuing Education:

Stay in touch with your field. Don't be satisfied with yesterday's accomplishments. Read trade journals, attend conferences and take refresher courses. Never stop learning or improving in your field. One of the realities of today is that technology and methods keep changing. If you fail to read books or magazines in your field of study or profession you may end up being left behind. In today's world, even mechanics have to learn about computer boards and sophisticated electronics. Stay in touch by reading, listening to and watching the latest in technology.

Chapter 5

Starting
a
Career

Employment

*B*y the sweat of your brow, you shall eat.' You may decide to go straight to work after high school and spend the rest of your life building a career. Alternatively, you can choose to work for a while and earn enough money to go to college or technical school. Suffice it to say that employment is both a good and mature option for you.

CAREER CHOICE GUIDELINES
Do not rush into choosing a career.

In senior high school, every student should be giving thought to a career choice but need not be settled on one. By the end of 12th grade, and certainly by the end of the first year in college, each student should have a pretty good idea of which career he or she wants to choose. Do not panic if you are graduating from high school or ending your first year of college and do not know your career choice. Many students experience the same thing. Just try to give it more careful thought.

Choosing a career is serious business because it will affect your life in the short term and in the long one. It will determine where you go, what you do, which courses you take, which school you attend and many other important factors in life. Since there are so many careers to choose from and so many factors that affect which career you should choose, there are some guidelines you should follow when considering a career. These guidelines are listed below

The choice of a career is one of the most important choices you will ever make in life. Choosing a career is as important as getting married, or where you are going to live and ranks with every other major decision you have to make in life. 'Why', you may ask? **The fact is most of us spend more time at work in our lives than at home. You will probably know more about the people you work with than some of your own family members.** You go to work eight to ten hours a day, five or six days a week. Work is a major part of your life. You go to work because you want food on your table and money to buy things. You go to work whether you like it or not as long as you get paid. So it is important to be pleased with your choice of career or you can end up leading an unfulfilled and miserable life.

In choosing a career you must know what you want. You need to know:

(a) What you want to be,
(b) Where you want to live,
(c) How you want to live and
(d) At what standard you want to live.

Your career must be planned or you could end up in a job you hate for the rest of your life. Here are the key considerations when it comes to choosing a career:

Know Yourself.

Many career persons find that their careers are incompatible with their life styles. Some people are extroverts (outgoing) and find careers that keep them away from people into what would be considered a boring existence. Other people are introverts (not outgoing) and are uncomfortable with careers that require them to do a lot of socializing. You must know yourself, your likes and dislikes, and try to choose a career that best suits you. This may not always be possible but try to choose a career that meets more of your likes than dislikes. Know yourself and what makes you tick, your talents, your strength and weaknesses, how you relate to people, and whether you have any existing preferences for a certain type of job. Be diligent and have a mind to work. Ask yourself the question, "What am I good at?" Take a look at what you are naturally good at. What are your strong points? What are you naturally interested in? Look at your talents and abilities and decide where your potential lies. It is easier to work toward your strengths than your weaknesses.

Count the Cost:

Decide what it will take for you to get from where you are to where you want to be. Decide if you are willing to sacrifice today for rewards that will come tomorrow. If you want to be a doctor, sacrifice comes with the package, eight to ten years of college and internships, numerous hours of study and less free time. If you want to be a clerk less study is required, if you want to pump gas even less is required. You must count the cost and determine how far you want to go.

Focus:

It is important to **focus** on your goals or your career. Don't allow yourself to be distracted. Basketball players, boxers or scientists often deny themselves things peers consider important for the sake of the goal. Many great basketball players have gone beyond the call of duty to put in extra practice, like shooting three hundred balls before a game in order to give them that extra edge. If you are to succeed you must be focused on your goal and avoid the things that will distract you. There are numerous opportunities for distractions out there so it is up to you to stay focused and avoid the distractions. Alcohol, drugs, promiscuity and bad relationships can all be distractions that rob you of your goal.

What is feasible in your environment?

Look at the trends in the country you live in and the environment or location you plan to spend your life. A rocket scientist may not be the best choice for the city or country you are in because there is no space program there. Speak to professionals or to your guidance counselor in order to determine what are the best fields or careers to get into. Some careers can be very limiting in a given environment. Seek an area that is likely to earn you money and is likely to be a growing field in the community where you live or where you desire to live.

Trends:

Computers and advanced technology are the order of the day. Many things are becoming obsolete today, so it is important to make that choice with good information. Take a look at what is happening in the business community and stay in touch with the trends. One of the best ways to do this is to occasionally read the weekly publication known as Business Week. This magazine looks at global trends in the field of business. Also read educational publications that deal with careers as well as your local newspaper or international newspaper. Stay in touch with what is happening in the world and be willing to adjust yourself to major trends in business and careers. There are also hundreds of websites that offer information on trends especially job sites.

Decide whether money or fulfillment is your priority.

Some careers pay a lot of money but do not give a sense of fulfillment (having done something meaningful). Others pay little, but give a sense of gratification. You must choose which is most important to you money or fulfillment. Once you do this, you can better make a career choice. Sometimes your career choice can offer both money and fulfillment. Other times, you can make a lot of money in a career that is not fulfilling and find fulfillment in other activities, or vice versa. In any case, it makes sense to give consideration to this factor. Compile a list of salaries for given careers and a list of social benefits that they offer. You can use the list to weigh each career according to your priorities.

Remember that a job is something we do for financial reward. A career is something we devote our lives to for fulfillment.

Let's look at what a career is all about:

The word career comes from the French word 'carriere'. It signifies the course and progress of a person's life. A career is a person's occupation that determines the course and progress of his or her life.

Explore as many careers as you can.

Read books, articles, papers and other material about as many different careers as you can. Talk to as many different career people as you can. Talk to people from each level of career development (clerk to manager). Ask them what they like most or like least about their career. Ask them what they had to do to get where they are. Ask them what educational skills and amount of experience were required. Ask as many questions as you can. Try to get a feel for their sense of satisfaction in their career choice.

You must determine whether or not you really want to work. Work is often not easy can always rewarding. Sometimes the reward is long in coming. Only if you have a mind to work, will you endure difficult times at work to wait for your reward. If you have a mind to work you will do what is necessary to equip yourself.

Remember also that one of your best experiences can be to work a summer job in your chosen field as this allows you to actually work in the environment you plan to make your career. Whether you are paid or not this is an excellent opportunity.

If you want to study the career market you can talk to persons from the following places:

Department of Labor & Human Resources
Chamber of Commerce
Various business houses
Local Libraries
School guidance counselors
School career counselors
Family members
Want Ads
Civic Organizations
Business Clubs
Church offices
Internet
College Fairs
Job Fairs

Wherever you can, you should also attend career development seminars, youth in business seminars, job fairs and other such programs.

Know what each career requires and whether you are prepared to meet those requirements. Most careers require many years of study, hard work and sacrifice. Some may require that you initially work long hours for little pay as an apprentice. Some may require that you work under very uncomfortable conditions for long periods of time. Some may require that you be away from home and your family for long periods. You must know what the career demands and decide whether or not you can meet that demand. Remember that the career into which you go is a matter of choice and not necessarily a reflection of your capabilities. It makes sense to go into a career where you can meet the demands and are likely to succeed, rather than one which will be too overwhelming for you.

The following is a list of things, among others, that you should know about a career:
- Opportunities that exist in the area, either now or in the future
- Academic qualifications required
- Number of years of experience required
- Terms of employment (salary, benefits, hours, vacation, leave, etc.)
- Type of responsibilities
- Opportunities for upward mobility (promotion)
- Level of social benefits

CAREER & VALUES

No career is worth having if it makes you compromise your values.

This issue is so important that it has to be dealt with separately. No matter what you do in life, even in choosing a career, you must bear in mind the impact it will have on your faith. By this I mean your belief system, your spiritual convictions, your moral standard and your religious beliefs. Everything that we do should positively affect our faith. It should please our consciences. It should give a sense of praise to God.

As you choose your career, pray to seek guidance. Jesus said, "Ask and you shall receive; seek and you shall find; knock and the door shall be opened to you". As you think about each career choice, ask yourself the question, *'is this choice consistent with my faith and belief system?'*

Chapter 6

Jobs
and
Employment

JOB SEARCH

The greatest treasures in life are found only after a long hard search.

A career is something to which you normally choose to devote most of your life, if not all. A career does not happen automatically. It must start with a first job. Your first job after school may have nothing to do with your career choice, even though it is good to start with one that does. Because the economy may not allow you to choose a job related to your career choice, you must be prepared to accept a job that is not. This does not mean that the job will be useless to you. Any legitimate job provides the following:

Honest money
Work experience working with others, following instruction, discipline etc.
Responsibility
Exposure to important people
Training

You must start somewhere and, believe me, a start is very important. You will only have one chance to make that first impression, so we want to give you a few tips that will help you to make your start a good one.

Challenges in Job Search.

As you search for a job you may find that no jobs are available at the time, or you do not have the necessary qualifications for the jobs that are available, or the pay for the available jobs is lower than you expected. Again the key is to be persistent and use the opportunity to better prepare yourself for the job when you get it. Even though there are people unemployed everywhere, some are unemployed because of their attitudes toward work and certain kinds of work. Every honest job is a good job, whether you get dirty or not. You can overcome these obstacles, if you stick with it.

WHERE DO YOU START?

Remember the list of contacts that we noted above as good places to study the career market? That same list is an important starting place in your job search. That list includes: Newspaper, Department of Labor, Internet, Internet Job Sites and your local Chamber of Commerce.

PREPARING A RÉSUMÉ

A résumé is very important to promoting yourself in the job market. A résumé also referred to as a C.V. (Curriculum Vitae), gives a summary of your academic and work experience. You do not have to be humble in preparing your résumé you just have to be honest. You should use your résumé to blow your own horn, for every accomplishment counts as an example of what you can do. Here is a sample résumé that you can follow in setting out your own résumé.

PERSONAL RÉSUMÉ OF

JOHN B. GOOD

JOHN B. GOOD

Address: 2601 NW 103RD ST
P.O. Box: CN1590 Nassau, Bahamas
Miami FL 33361
Telephone (542) 323-0000

Date of Birth:
1 January, 1980

Place of Birth:
Nassau, Bahamas

Citizenship: Bahamian/American

Height:

Weight: 180 lbs.

Marital Status:
Single

No. of Children:
None

Notify in Case of Emergency:
Mother
Mary I.S. Good

100 Nowhere Street
Nassau, Bahamas.

Telephone:
(542) 325-0000

EDUCATION

Coconut Elementary School 1984-1989
Mango High School 1989-1993

Accomplishments
GPA 4.0
Diploma with Honors /GED/ 5 B.J.C.
5 B.G.C.S.E.

University of Florida
Bachelor of Science Degree in Computer Engineering

JOB EXPERIENCE

1999-2000   Fantastic Homes Ltd. Summer employee
               Responsibilities: Gopher/Filing Clerk

1997-1998   Build it Construction Ltd.
               Summer employee

Responsibilities:
Cement mixer

1996   Bakers & Barbers
            Summer employee
            Responsibilities:
            Pastry chef

PERSONAL ACCOMPLISHMENTS

STUDENT COUNCIL PRESIDENT   1989-1993 Mango High School
President: Junior Achievers (1992)
Sr. Basketball team: Captain (1993)
Principals List   (1989-1993)
President: Student Government (1993)

PERSONAL INTERESTS

Basketball, travel, public speaking, community work, reading, social activism.

PERSONAL ATTRIBUTES

Articulate, organized, leadership skills, friendly, personable, sensible.

REFERENCES: Available upon request.

You can use this format to fill in details about your own life. Try to find someone with a computer to assist you in preparing the résumé. There are many companies that provide this type service (e.g. Kinko's, Office Depot or Office Max, Staples). A good-looking résumé is the best way to make a notable first impression. There are also computer programs that assist with Resume preparation.

Employment

Most qualified persons who seek a job will find one. Under the best economic conditions, about ninety-four to ninety six percent (94% - 96%) of such people would be employed; a condition known as full employment. In bad economic conditions the employment rate can be as low as 80%. Still it means that either nine out of ten persons will be employed or eight out of ten.

Despite the large number of employed persons, there are those who are unemployed. That is, there are people who are actively looking for a job but cannot find one. The rate of unemployment varies from time to time. Jobs can be found in the manufacturing, e-commerce, hospitality industry, banking, construction, wholesale and retail trades. The government employs many persons as well.

Self-employment:

One option that is often not considered or pursued aggressively but that is very viable as far as a career is concerned is the option of self-employment. Self- employment for many is a much better option than entering the work force since you can control your own destiny and there is no limit on your earning ability. Of course self-employment involves taking risks but that is a part of business and is an integral part of business *and* progress. Not everyone is cut out to be self- employed so this is an important issue to consider. You may want to pursue your own business or start out working in a field and then branch out into your own business. It is vitally important that you count the cost and assess your personality before you decide to become a business owner. Many people are not suited to self-employment; they require supervision and are driven by others rather than self-driven.

If you are considering self employment the most important tool to be aware of is a BUSINESS PLAN which helps you to outline your potential business and investment risks and rewards. Consulting a lawyer and accountant are also of vital importance so that you may prepare financial projections and prepare for incorporation.

Chapter 7

Money, Money, Money

Understanding Economics & Trade

Some economies are what we call service based. For example, the Bahamas sells services (tourism, banking, haircuts, etc.) rather than products (cars, computers, garments, toys, etc.). Our primary economic activities are tourism and financial services. Tourism accounts for approximately 70% of what we earn as a country while financial services or banking accounts for about 15%. Most of the jobs and money we have in The Bahamas come as a result of these areas of the economy. Tourism and banking, however, are becoming more challenged to sustain the country's growth and development on their own. Other countries rely on a products based economy where the majority of jobs come from manufacturing and production. The United States has a diversified economy and depending upon the region you live in, the economy can be a service economy or a production and manufacturing based economy. Other sectors of economy are made up of wholesale and retail trade, construction, real estate, agriculture, fisheries, and government activities. A growing trend in the world market is e-commerce as many individuals now compete with large companies simply by having a web presence and online store.

International Trade

International trade involves buying goods and services from the rest of the world and selling goods and services *to* the rest of the world. When we buy from the world it is called importing and when we sell to the world it is called exporting. Some countries buy more goods from other countries than they buy from themselves. This would make up an import-based economy. In our tourism based economy we sell more tourism services to the rest of the world than they sell to us. So the money we earn from tourism helps us pay for the goods and services we buy from other countries. We buy mostly from the USA, China, Canada, the United Kingdom and Japan.

Money

Each country has its own currency; in many countries it is called the dollar.

The Bahamian dollar is on par with the US dollar. That is, one Bahamian dollar can be traded for one US dollar. The stability of the dollar depends on our ability to earn foreign currency, maintain a low, stable inflation rate and stable interest rates. So far, we are able to earn sufficient foreign reserves, keep our inflation rate low, and maintain reasonable interest rates in order to keep the Bahamian dollar's parity with that of the U.S.A.

The National Debt

Like almost all countries, the United States and The Bahamas has a national debt. In order for the Government to provide public goods and services, it must earn revenue through taxes and fees. When the Government spends more than it earns, it must borrow money. It borrows this money locally and internationally by issuing bonds or direct borrowing from banks. It also borrows money from international financial institutions such as the Inter American Development Bank (IDB) and the World Bank. The total amount of money the Government and its organizations owe is known as the national debt. Like any loan, the principal and interest must be paid on time. Government pays these with the revenue it raises but in our case, it is primarily done by import duties. In other countries it may be raised by income taxes, state taxes, sales taxes or real property taxes. Each year there is an amount placed in the budget to make the loan payments arising from the national debt. One way to look at the national debt is to think of it as the amount of money all of us owe for the borrowing the Government has done over the years. We will all pay it back as the Government taxes us to make the loan payments.

Money, Money, Money

Contrary to popular opinion, money is not the root of all evil. Mismanaging money may be closer on the list of being the root of all evil. Actually, the statement that comes from the Bible says that "the love or obsession with money is the root of evil", because when your life consists of living to hoard money it can become a miserable existence. However we look at it, dealing with money at any age is important.

One of the biggest, if not the biggest problem in marriage, is the handling of money. Money and sex cause more problems in marriage than any other items. One of the reasons there are so many problems in marriages as it relates to money is that persons did not learn to handle money as teenagers or young adults. They are not taught early in life how to budget and invest so when they enter a marriage the bad habits they have learned end up causing conflicts in their marriages.

Money is an important matter. Money is vitally important. In the book of Ecclesiastes the Bible indicates that "money answers all things", meaning all tangible things on earth. If money is the answer to the temporal things of our existence then we must learn how to handle money. What we will explain below is how to handle money effectively for your benefit in order to answer the questions of your day-to-day financial existence. Let's look at how we should handle money.

a) Learn to Budget - No matter how much money you have or don't have budgeting is important. A budget is a guide to dealing with money successfully. If you grow up in the habit of not budgeting it is very likely that you will take your bad habit into adult life or marriage. In order to help you to understand budgeting, I have included below a family budget and then a personal budget. The basics of budgeting are recognizing your income and expenses and making decisions that keep you from spending more than you earn yet allowing you to save or invest. If you learn to budget the little you have now, when you end up with much more responsibilities it will be much easier.

Family Budget

Income Items

Salary	$2,500.00
Business Income	$ 100.00
Other Income	$ 300.00
Bonus	$ 175.00
Side Job	$ 5 0.00
Dividends	$ 100.00
Total Income	**$3,225.00**

Expense Items

Tithes	$ 322.50
Mortgage	$1,000.00
Credit Cards	$ 205.00
Clothes	$ 250.00
Utilities	$ 400.00
Insurances	$ 200.00
Loans	$ 350.00
Gas/Car	$ 125.00
Savings	$ 121.00
Recreation	$ 60.00
Entertainment	$ 60.00

Totals Expenses   **$3, 093.00**

Net Income   **$132.00**

With this budget you end up with a savings of $132.00. This helps in making budgeting decisions. It means you will have to reduce something in the future in order to save more and maintain a (surplus) budget. This is what budgeting is all about, making decisions based upon information. Monitoring your spending every month and making adjustments where necessary is also an integral part of budgeting.

Personal Youth Budget

Income Items

Salary (Part Time)	$500.00
Allowances	$100.00
Other Income	$300.00

Total Income   **$900.00**

Expense Items
Tithes	$90.00

Lunch/Food	$100.00
Clothes	$150.00
Transportation	$125.00
Savings	$75.00
Recreation	$60.00
Entertainment	$60.00
Miscellaneous	$100.00
Total Expenses	**$760.00**
Net Income	**$140.00**

In this budget you end up with a savings of $140.00. What should you do with this surplus the following month? Do you buy an expensive gift for your girlfriend, a pair of expensive footwear or do you put it in your savings account for now until you decide how to allocate it? Do you use it to save for college? These are budgeting decisions on the personal level. The decisions you make now affect your future. Perhaps you may want to devise your own budget using this format or one you developed yourself. In any event, consult with a family member who is an accountant, a financial consultant or banker and ask for their help. If your parents prepare budgets ask them to help as well.

b) Learn to Save - Never spend all of your money. Open a bank account and learn to put some of your money away for future investments. Do not spend all of your money on clothes or entertainment. Save for college, important personal items or things you need to advance yourself. As a guideline begin to practice saving at least 10% of your income.

c) Learn to Invest - Saving is good but often the interest you earn is not very high. Other investments often yield a higher return. For example, investing in stocks and bonds can bring you higher returns. Investing in your own business can also bring a good return. It is important that you speak with someone who is qualified and attends money management and investment seminars in order to gain a good understanding of investment. Most of the wealthy people in the world are investors.

d) Always buy property - (real estate) before you buy a new car. A new car can depreciate by 30% over the first three years. Real estate increases in value each year. You cannot live in a car and neither can your family.

Invest in your future. Buy a good used car instead of a new one until you own real estate. This is vitally important when you are young because if you want to build a home the first thing the bank will ask for is collateral. Real estate is one of the best forms of collateral. Owning real estate will help you to avoid the trap of using most of your income when you are young to pay off someone else's mortgage by paying rent for years. If you are going to spend money, spend it on your own mortgage rather than rent. As you pay your mortgage you build equity and eventually you will own your home or apartment. If you build an apartment and get finished with paying the mortgage, it becomes an investment that can earn you money for the rest of your life.

KEY FACTORS TO CONSIDER

The simple points above about the economy and managing money should make you aware of what you must face as you explore life after high school. The challenges pointed out are real and they can affect the opportunities that you are afforded. Basically, the key factors to consider from the information given are the following:

You must understand how the economy works.

You must learn how to budget and invest money

Entrepreneurship offers one of the best prospects for creating new jobs and wealth in the future.

Traditional trades (farming, fishing, carpentry, plumbing, mechanics, etc.) can be excellent opportunities for growth and development, especially if excellence is the code by which the trades are operated.

Opportunities for government employment will continue to decline due to the need for government to reduce its size, in order to balance its budget and enhance the economic growth of the country.

You should be sure to study your economy further. Know where opportunities are and where they can be created. You can prosper and excel, it's really up to you.

Chapter 8

Priorities of Life

Body Priorities

As I stated earlier we are made up of three parts. Spirit, Soul and Body. The 'least' important, if you could use such a term, is the body. But that does not mean the body is not important. In fact there is a direct correlation between all the parts that make up "you". A messed up body affects the mind, a messed up mind affects the spirit, a messed up spirit affects body and mind.

The million dollar question then is, 'how do I make plans for my body?' One of the first and most important items is to plan to protect your body from its enemies. The world that we live in is a very interesting place. We promote lies as truth to the point that teenagers never understand until years later how convincing the lie was and how much it cost them. **A lie heard 1,000 times sounds a lot better than the truth heard once.** One of the lies advertised very effectively every day is that you need drugs or alcohol. These things steal life and years from you. How do I know?

After years of drug use from marijuana to cocaine to beer to wine, I (Pastor Dave) damaged my body and robbed it of its best years. As I got older and stopped using drugs, I finally realized what it had done to my friends and I. Some of them went crazy, literally crazy because of drug use, others had their lives and careers cut short. Some, including me, had damage done that sometimes is not so obvious: memory loss, problems with sleeping, and loss of ability. Plan to keep your life free of all drugs whether in the bottle or the can. Beer is no different than marijuana or cocaine. They all kill in one way or another. Intoxication in any form is not a good thing. Many alcohol companies remind you to drink responsibly, meaning that it is easy to be irresponsible with alcohol. This also means that you are better off without it.

Plan to keep physically fit. Many young people take it for granted that because they are young and strong they need not pay attention to their bodies. If your body is a temple that God wants to live in it pays not to allow your body to get out of shape. Every athlete (if he wants to win his race or play his best) disciplines himself in order to be at his best. If you want to be at your best it is important to keep yourself fit, and important to have an exercise plan. This is true whether you are male or female.

Hit the weight room, run, play ball, walk, swim or do whatever it takes to keep yourself in physical shape. Develop a regular routine and you will find that a physically fit person can study better, is more alert and is more likely to be a winner in life. Physical fitness is one of the keys to fitness in other areas of your life.

Plan to eat right. Some may say what do you mean eat right? Is there a right and wrong way to eat? There is a right and wrong in everything and the right way leads to good things while the wrong way leads to bad things. If you eat right your chances of staying healthy and living long are increased. If you eat wrong it can kill you at an early age. Eating right means using the foods that will give you the greatest benefit and advantage. Wrong foods cause you to lose your health. Over and over again studies seem to keep proving that eating foods in their natural state is better. It is important to eat high fiber foods, honey, nuts and bran products. It has been stated that a diet of fruits and vegetables, limited meat or no meat at all, no or very little refined (white) sugar and salt, no junk food and no high cholesterol is the best way to eat. Junk food products often taste good but can be harmful to your health. We all love the taste of fast food pizza, hamburgers or fried chicken, but often these are not the best foods to eat. Get information on food, speak to a nutritionist and find out what foods are best for you. Develop a diet that works to your advantage. If you fail to do it now you will get into bad eating habits and end up in a doctor's office trying to correct problems that you could have avoided. Also check the labeling on packages detailing the nutritional content. Almost all food packages now carry nutritional content information.

Plan not to abuse your body and violate the laws set in place by God. You have to plan, young lady, not to get pregnant. Someone out there has a plan for your body and that plan is to infect it with AIDS, to get you pregnant and to kill you or make your life miserable. This person may look good or have a nice smile or drive a nice, nice car. AIDS is not very discriminating; it will infect anyone. AIDS carriers do not carry nametags or identification cards. **If you don't want AIDS or want to get pregnant you have to make the decision not to give others access to your body. You have to establish standards that you use as a measuring stick. If someone does not respect your standards that person is against you and should be treated like an enemy.**

Many people in the world have concluded that teenagers cannot help but become sexually active. While it is very difficult in a sexually charged world it is not impossible. You can abstain and it is the best decision you can make. Wait now and enjoy later or take the shortcut and pay for the rest of your life. If you want to abstain from sex it will not work at 5.00 a.m. in the morning on a couch somewhere or parked in the dark with the music turned down low. Do not allow yourself to be in the wrong situations, nor should you allow anyone to touch you under your clothes or arouse you sexually. **Sex is never free. Sex always comes with consequences or excess baggage. Sex and marriage go together, sex and babies go together, sex and family go together, sex and bills, sex and diapers, sex and babies crying in the night. Sex is never free or easy, there is always a price tag attached.** Sex is meant to be enjoyed in the right environment.

Many young people make the mistake of making lovers out of what should be friends. It is much more important as a youth to concentrate on learning the differences between males and females and learning how to treat ladies or young men with respect. You should learn to treat the opposite sex as a brother or sister. There is nothing wrong with communication and interaction but it is so much more important to learn how to be a lady or a gentleman, simple things that will make your life better. I grew up (Pastor Dave) only learning to abuse young ladies and thought they loved me regardless of what I did. I was mean, only looked out for myself and did not do simple things like pull a chair for a lady if we went out, or open her door and treat her with respect. One of your greatest aims as a young person should be learning how to be a gentleman or a lady. As I got older and wiser I began to realize the importance of these things. When you get married you will find that a lady prefers a gentleman. You can accomplish much more and be better equipped for marriage if you learn to treat the opposite sex with respect, rather than as a piece of property or sex object.

Another important lesson for teenagers is to understand the physical differences between males and females. Many times young people assume many things about the opposite sex and end up getting hurt because of it. Most teenagers do not know what I am about to explain and many suffer because of it. Young men and young ladies are distinctly different. The male hormone is testosterone. This hormone makes the male naturally more aggressive than the female. The male is designed to pursue. He is stimulated by sight and wants every girl he sees (or feels like it). Most males stand and stare as females pass, analyzing their figures and thinking what it would be like if they could get their hands on this lady. Young ladies sometimes believe the young man is interested in them romantically when, in actuality, his hormones are driving his interest on a purely sexual basis. Most young men just want a good time.

Young ladies, on the other hand, are influenced by the hormone estrogen. God gives this hormone to make the female different from the male. Estrogen causes a young lady to be less aggressive and to want to receive love and attention. It causes her to want a relationship. She is stimulated much more slowly than a young man and instead of being stimulated simply by staring at a male she tends to be convinced by words and actions. If a young man complements her or pays attention to her over a period of time then she responds, she wants security and relationship whereas he only wants a good time. The result of these two coming together is often tragic. Good time (young male) has a good time, relationship (young female) ends up with a baby and still no relationship. It is therefore even more important for young ladies to realize the makeup of young men and protect themselves from this syndrome that leaves so many young ladies with babies and no father for the baby. This is another reason why it is much better not to focus on romantic relationships early in your teen years. It is better to wait and to focus your teen years on having fun and relating to the opposite sex but not getting into deep emotional relationships. Concentrate on you and developing your interactive skills rather than relationships.

If you allow others access to your body you mess up your future and open yourself to problems. Sexually transmitted diseases are a reality and kissing is not a harmless recreational activity. AIDS and other diseases can be transmitted through many different types of sexual activity. If you kiss someone who has the AIDS virus and they happened to brush their teeth and bled slightly from their gum, you can catch AIDS. It is possible although not likely.

Plan to discipline your body. Your body is God's temple. Athletes discipline their bodies in order to be the best they can be for a competition. They have camps to get their bodies in top shape. Basketball players run, exercise and lift weights in order to be their best. Runners discipline themselves for a goal; they watch what they eat because they want to be in the best shape for the competition. You do not have to be an athlete to realize the importance of physical discipline. It pays to keep in good physical shape. I discovered years ago that I study better and fall asleep less when I am in good physical shape.

A quote from the Bible encourages us to **"flee youthful lusts"**. If it says to flee or run away from youthful lusts there must be some lusts that are particularly applicable to youth. Young people who are looking for adventure are easy prey to youthful lusts. Sex before marriage, drugs, gangs, excessive partying are all things that 'afflict' young people. The easiest time period in life to waste time and spend your days pursuing unrestrained pleasure is when you are young. The older you get the more settled you become and the less tempted you are by 'youthful lusts'. As a teenager you must realize that these temptations exist and prepare to run away from them.

Your body has appetites. Never trust your body to give you direction in life. You have to tell your body what to do or it will betray you. Your body often wants to eat junk food and sleep. If you listen to it your body you will end up fat and out of shape. Tell your body what it needs to do. If you wait until you get older it may be too late. **Your greatest opportunity to set the record straight and to develop the right habits for your body is in your youth.**

Spiritual Priorities

Most people in the world think of only two areas of life: Body and Mind. Sometimes it is easy to plan for the body and the mind. Many never consider the third part to each human being. The Spirit is that third part and is actually the most important. The Bible is the basis of much of what we are talking about in this book and it clearly indicates that we are three part beings. We are spirit. The spirit is the real person. When our bodies are no longer, our spirit is the thing that remains. The Bible also indicates that God is a spirit and if we want to worship him we must do so in spirit; spirit to Spirit. **Because the spirit is not tangible we often don't think of spirit as important. Yet the spirit is the most important. Many people only prepare for body and mind and neglect the need for spiritual preparation.** It is vitally important as a young person to consider your spiritual direction because it often is the difference between life and death. There are some spiritual and existential questions that we must ask. All of us need to ask why are we here on this earth? Is there a God and what does he require of us? Should we give our lives to him? Is there life after death? What effect does the spiritual have on the tangible in life?

These questions can only be answered on an individual basis. You cannot have a group to decide these questions for you. You must decide on a personal level. I came to a point in my life as a young man (Pastor Dave) where I concluded that I did believe in God but was not serving him or paying attention to him. Although it was a difficult process I came to the conclusion that there was a God and that I needed to come to terms with him, rather than running away and messing up my life. In the end I received new direction and achieved a much better life only after I gave my life to God and asked him to help me run it. I came to the conclusion that Jesus Christ, through the Bible, and a personal relationship with him held the answers to my deepest questions. I concluded that if I did believe in God then it was my duty to do what he said and live the way he prescribed in the Bible. So the spiritual question or questions must be answered by all of us. I cannot do it for you or tell you what you have to do; you must answer these questions for yourself.

Many young people believe that serving God means taking away their fun but the truth is this concept is only a result of constant misrepresentation of God. Some young people think God is there and does not want them to enjoy life. But the Bible says that Jesus came that we might have life more abundant and full (John 10:10).

We should love, yet be strong. We should live without the distraction of unrestrained or unproductive living. We are supposed to have the same mind like Christ. We are supposed to live right and this is the foundation for success. You should pay great attention to the spiritual aspect of life. What does it profit a man if he gains the whole world yet loses his soul?

Set spiritual goals for your life.

A very logical question may be, 'how do I set spiritual goals?' Here are some tips:

First you must be committed to spiritual development and growth.

Never be content with your spiritual state. Make progress in every area of your life. Once you have committed your life the next step is to be planted and grow. To grow means you must understand what the Kingdom of God is and what the objectives of this Kingdom are. Jesus prayed his kingdom come and his will be done on earth. Our job is to learn the principles of his kingdom and to ensure that we live by them and advance these objectives on the earth. In order to advance God's plan we must become a part of his system, which is to belong to a local church that is living by and practicing these principles. The next step is to be a personal ambassador and have your life be an example to others. Once you understand what God says and what he wants you to do it is then your job to go out and do it regardless of whether other young people agree with you or understand you. If you are right no apologies are necessary. You are a personal witness of something you have settled in your own heart. Just do it!

It is very important to just relax and grow in your faith. Read, pray, study and witness under the guidance of your local church and youth group. Everyone in this world is spouting some philosophy at you every day. People may accuse you of being religious if your share your faith, yet they share their beliefs with you everyday in song, in word, in movies. Movie directors have a philosophy that comes out in their movies; teachers in school have a personal philosophy that comes out in the classroom. **You have a right to share your personal faith with anyone. They have the right to respond however they would like.** While you are a young person it is the best time to become strong in your faith. Many people wait until they have wasted their years in foolish living like the prodigal son then come back home only after being abused by this world. It is better to take advantage of the good things God has to offer you now than to come to him later for a repair job.

It is a fact that we are living in dangerous times. The world gets more complicated and difficult by the day. Decide to make continual progress in your spiritual life. Do not be content just to be a Christian. Decide to become a mature person moving from the elementary things to the deeper things. Young people die everyday by the bullet of a gun, the needle, suicide and AIDS, full of unused potential. It is up to you to be the one who stands out from the crowd. Be full of the image of God. If you are a young person today do not wait until tomorrow. Plan to grow from one level to a higher level spiritually.

Remember that you can only develop your spirit by reading, meditating and praying. Meditate on what you have read and listened to from your local Church or your local Christian bookstore. Pray and learn more about how to pray and how to achieve results praying. The Bible contains the instructions for living. This is the only manual provided by the manufacturer. We must have a good understanding of our directions for life. The Bible is also our 'Constitution', containing our bill of rights and orders from our President. If you believe in God you must believe that he has a plan for your life and decide to follow that plan to the letter. The better you follow the plan the better your life will be.

Chapter 9

Wisdom
Tips

In summing up what is important in the teen years there are some key areas that can make a big difference in your future. What follows is a list of areas that, in addition to what we have already covered, can have a big impact on your success or failure during the teen years and beyond. Here are some tips on making the most of your young life.

Key #1 Have Fun

Some people cringe at the idea of enjoying life. Some people expect teenagers to be too serious. Enjoy your teen years. Learn to enjoy life and have fun. Listen to good positive music; get involved in sports, drama, watch good movies and party with friends in a wholesome and clean environment. Fun has for so long been associated with drunkenness or drugs or sexual promiscuity that we sometimes forget that you can have just as much or more fun without those things. Make sure that you enjoy your teen years because they will soon be gone, never to return again. If you develop the right principles and standards from the beginning you can let your standards guide your future.

Key #2 Be Friendly

One of the most important things about being a teenager is developing relationships. It is very important to be friendly to others. You learn more by having access to more people. Friends are an opportunity to meet people, learn things about life and have a good time. Learn not to be selfish with your life. Opportunities for growth come with learning to relate to others in non-emotional relationships. Jesus, who was our greatest example, made friends with all kinds of people. In fact the Bible states that people accused him of associating with "sinners and publicans". Yet he never became like the people he associated with. He always influenced others for good.

Key #3 Set Your Own Agenda

Many young people tend to be followers, following an agenda set by someone else. Peer pressure, fashion, music, movies and television all have an agenda that comes from the ones who create these products. You must decide what your agenda is and make sure that you are the one who influences rather than the one being influenced. Be a leader. Create things for others to follow. Be the one to suggest what should be done rather than the one who always follows other suggestions. In your high school decide to be the leader of your social, civic or athletic group. Leaders have more power to influence for good. You be the one to start a Bible study or music group. You be the one to invite others to an event you are involved in. Remember to avoid crowds. Eagles fly alone, turkeys flock together and end up on the dinner table.

Key #4 Respect Authority

Learn to respect authority. Many teenagers are influenced by a popular culture that encourages young people to be disrespectful to parents and authority figures. One day you will have a family and want respect from your children. Learn to respect authority because God sets up authority to keep order. If you grow up being disrespectful to those older than you, you can stunt your own growth. What goes around comes around (they say), and this is true when it comes to respect. Learn common "manners" because these things help you to get ahead in life and eventually you would want people to have the same respect for you. Give honor to who it is due.

Key #5 Develop Right Relationships

This may seem to be trivial and many times we get the feeling that love conquers all but as you get older it is important to develop relationships that will benefit you. The way to do this is to make friends and associate with people who have similar goals. This may not seem important now but if you ever end up in a marriage only to realize that you never had the same goals or the same agenda in life it could be disastrous. Your friends should be people who are going in the same direction you are going in. Your girlfriend or boyfriend should be someone who shares your beliefs, goals and dreams. To develop relationships with people who are going in the opposite direction can cause great difficulty. If you are interested in educating yourself via a college education and your boyfriend or girlfriend wants to pump gas at a local gas station that is not a right or good relationship. You can have acquaintances at all levels but your close friends should be similar to you in their goals and aspirations.

MAKE YOUR CONTRIBUTION

If we walk through the sands of time and leave no footprints, we are no different than those who have never been born. A key word for new graduates to remember is contribution. It should be your determination to make a contribution to your family, your neighborhood, your community and your country.

Most of us seek to be successful people. That is, we want to have a respectable job that pays well. We want to be noted as persons of influence in the society. We want to have a nice home and car and we want to live comfortably. While there is nothing wrong with wanting these things, we must also remember that we have a responsibility to help build our communities. After all, as we build up our community we create better opportunities for ourselves and others.

You can be a leader in civics, education, business, religion and politics. There are many nontraditional organizations that look for people to assist. Young and bright people are extremely useful to service organizations, charities and churches. You should seek to devote some of your energies to these groups.

TIME TO WAKE UP

More important than the difficulty you face is the response you make to that difficulty. I wish that I could tell you that your life after school will be easy but I cannot. Remember, this is supposed to be straight talk. It is very likely that things will happen differently than you expect. Even with the important tips that you are being given, you will come to discover that things may still not be easy, but you can make it.

Avoid Unnecessary Distractions.

There are many things in this world that distract us from pursuing our goals. Often times, people who do not mean us well try to persuade us to do things we ought not to do or go places that we ought not to go. Sometimes these people are called our friends. You must remember that a friend will make you sharp and not dull. A friend will seek the best for you and not only what appears to be fun for you. You must be sure that the people you hang out with are going somewhere worthwhile and want to be decent people.

Wanting to have fun can also be a distraction. It's good to have fun but you must have fun the right way and at the right time. When it is time to work you should not try to have fun, unless you can make your work fun. Everything has its time.

Be careful of illegal drugs, alcohol use, sexual misconduct, violence and other things that can distract you or hurt you. Seek opportunities to do good and improve your life daily. The decision is always yours.

THINK ETERNITY

Life is more than right now. The greatest way to succeed in life is to live knowing that some day we must give account.

Many people live as if they have no future, as if there is no tomorrow. For that reason they make careless decisions; they fail to save; they commit crimes and the like. When you know that there is a tomorrow you are patient, recognizing that you might not enjoy things now but you may enjoy them later. You must make the kind of decisions today that will make things better for you tomorrow. This might mean sacrificing some fun today but it may also mean more fun tomorrow.

You should also know that what you see is not all there is to life. There is a spiritual world that you cannot see. This spiritual world is important because it lasts forever. Everything that you see around you will some-day fade away. The things that are spiritual, like God, angels and your human spirit will last forever. Because the spiritual will last forever, we should pay more attention to it. Just as you and I were born, some day we will also die. Between birth and death is what we call life. We must live life in such a way that our birth is worthwhile and our death is mean-ingful. If we live our lives obedient to God, helpful to others and fulfilling to ourselves, we will have lived a good life. When we die, we will go on to the best life, for we will spend eternity with God.

If I can leave anything with you it is this. Keep your priorities in the right order. Learn from the example of those who have gone before and don't repeat their mistakes. Remember to plan for your spirit, soul and body. Remember that none of us can save the world but we can save ourselves. We cannot change our friends but we can change our own direction. Get the maximum out of life by putting God first in your life and by planning for your future.

Conclusion

The world we live in today is continually changing. It is becoming more and more difficult for young people to stay alive long enough to become adults. It seems that too little instructions are given to young people about the practical aspects of life. There is reading, writing and arithmetic but little about how to prepare for life ahead. The things we have shared in this book are designed to deal with how to prepare for life ahead. Not everything about this subject has been included in this book but there is enough for you to change the way you look at life and to make the necessary adjustments you need to make to ensure a brighter future.

The sad truth about this present life is that it seems more and more young people are being persuaded to throw their lives away. Do not join the crowd that is intent on living a mediocre existence, simply waiting for the next party or the next high. You need to decide that you will get the most out of your teen years now and as time goes on, be prepared for what lies ahead in the way of family and career.

About
the
Authors

Minister the Honorable Zhivargo Laing

Zhivargo Laing, son of straw vendor Naomi Seymour and former hotel worker, the late Cedric Laing was born on September 7, 1967, in Nassau, but grew up in Freeport.

He received his early education at Lewis Yard Primary School and Hawksbill High School where he was Head Boy. Later he attended the College of The Bahamas and was elected President of the College of The Bahamas Union of Students.

Zhivargo completed studies leading to a Bachelor of Arts Degree in Economics from the University of Western Ontario in Canada. Later he undertook graduate studies at the George Washington University. He also received training in foreign investment promotion in Taiwan and Japan.

In May 1997, Mr. Laing was elected to the House of Assembly as the Free National Movement's representative for the Fort Charlotte constituency. He was appointed Minister of State in Youth, Sports, & Culture, Minister of State in Education, and Minister of Economic Development. He was re-elected to Parliament as the representative for the Free National Movement for the Marco City Constituency in May 2007, and was appointed as Minister of State in the Ministry of Finance.

Zhivargo is the author of three books: "College, Career and Money – A Guide for Teens & Young Adults," "A Trust Out of this World" and "Who Moved My Conch – Understanding How Free Trade will affect the Bahamian Economy." He wrote a weekly column "Straight Up Talk" for the Tribune and was the host of "Public Affairs Corner", and a radio talk show on Mix 102.1 FM. He was the proprietor of Pro-Life Development Systems, a motivational speaking, training, and business consulting firm.

A member of the Assemblies of God Churches, Mr. Laing is married to the former Zsa Zsa Monique LaRoda and they have three sons, Zhivargo II, Zhimaal and Zavier, and one daughter Za'riah.

Pastor Dave "Davy B" Burrows

Pastor Dave Burrows affectionately known as "Davy B" was born and raised in Nassau, Bahamas and grew up as a troubled teenager on the streets, spending his teen years as a rebellious youth involved in the street world of drugs, violence, sexual promiscuity and crime. After several close encounters with the law, Dave through the influence of his brother-in-law Pastor Robyn Gool of Charlotte North Carolina, accepted Christ and went on to graduate from Oral Roberts University.

He later worked for the Bahamas Government in the Ministry of Youth and Sports where he orchestrated many highly successful programs for youth. One of the foremost authorities in the world on Youth Ministry, Pastor Dave Burrows is a Youth Ministry specialist, President of Youth Alive Ministries and founder and president of The Christian Youth Leaders Network and the Global Youth Ministry Leadership Network. With over 25 years of experience in Youth Ministry Dave has pioneered many successful programs for youth affecting gangs, youth from all backgrounds, youth leaders around the world and Churches, Pastors and entire organizations and denominations.

In addition to his own organization Dave Burrows Youth and Family Inc, he currently serves as Pastor of TYC (Total Youth Church) and president of Youth Alive Ministries a subsidiary of Bahamas Faith Ministries International headed by Dr. Myles Munroe. Dave has revolutionized youth ministry in the Bahamas and many areas of the world through a variety of unconventional programs that have impacted, gangs, drug users, troubled youth as well as everyday young people. His methods and down to earth approach have earned him the nickname "The Ruffneck Pastor".

Pastor Dave travels, locally within the Bahamas and internationally as a conference speaker, motivating youth, churches, youth ministries and school groups to maximize their God given potential. He has been a speaker or conducted seminars for: Crenshaw Christian Center (Dr. Fredrick Price), West Angeles Church of God in Christ (Bishop Charles Blake), Victory Christian Center (Pastor Robyn Gool, North Carolina) Youth With a Mission, Oral Roberts University, Youth for Christ, Christ For the Nations as well as churches and conferences throughout the Caribbean,

North America, Canada and Europe.

Dave has authored eight books including Sex & Dating, Making the Most of Your Teenage Years, Strategies for Saving the Next Generation, Talk to Me, Kingdom Parenting and College Career and Money, and has produced or served as executive producer for four movies "Dear Diary", "Kim", "X Factor" and "Metamorphosis" and two CD Music compilations featuring Caribbean Gospel in contemporary styles including Reggae and Hip Hop. He has also hosted TV and radio programs including "The Ruffneck Myxx", "Effective Youth" and "Talk to Me" and the Youth and Family show which currently airs on JCN TV in the Bahamas.

Pastor Dave has appeared on many television and radio programs world-wide including programs hosted by TBN, Richard Roberts (Hour of Healing) and TD Jakes (Potters Touch) and has also served as a contributing writer for many Christian Publications. He has served as an advisor to the Bahamas Government on Youth Matters, having three times served as chairman of the National Youth Advisory Council and has served on the Family Life and Health advisement group.

Dave Burrows has also founded programs for male mentorship "Young Champions", Christian School clubs "Christ 4 Life" and a young ladies mentorship program spearheaded by his wife Angela "P31". Pastor Dave also has hosted many major events for teens, parents and youth workers that attract thousands including the annual Youth Alive Conference which attracts up to 6,000 persons both from the Bahamas and world-wide. Pastor Dave is credited with helping thousands of teens from troubled backgrounds to make positive turnarounds or achieve their leadership potential. He has also motivated youth to achieve great personal and professional accomplishments through his motivational and inspirational events in schools and colleges.

In addition to his ministry work, Dave Burrows is also an avid business-man as the owner of Megabyte Computers and One Rib Publishing Company. He conducts many motivational and business seminars for corporations, organizations and businesses and has released a series titled "Starting a Business and Maximizing Technology". He is also President and CEO of the business and motivational organization "The Winners Touch". His wife Angela ministers along with him and runs the family businesses. Pastor Dave & Angela have two children, Arri and Davrielle.

JOB WEBSITES: www.monster.com, www.job.com, www.careerbuilder. com, www.theladders.com

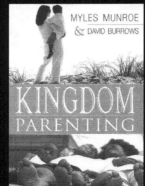
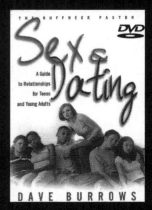

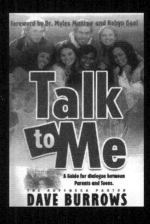
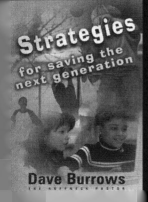
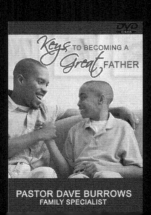
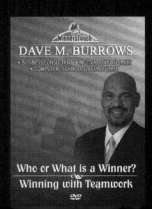